Poems of Lu Hsun

魯迅詩歌

黄新渠

譯注

POEMS OF LU HSUN

Translated and annotated by
Huang Hsin-chyu

2nd Edition

Joint Publishing Co.
Hongkong. 1981

First Published in July 1979
Second Edition, September 1981

Printed in Hongkong by
C & C Joint Printing Co. (H. K.) Ltd.
75 Pau Chung Street, Kowloon, Hongkong

ISBN 962.04.0010.0

Portrait by Tao Yuan-ching

Lu Hsun in 1902, in Tokyo, Japan

Picture of Lu Hsun,

taken on his fiftieth birthday

Lu Hsun, Bernard Shaw and Tsai Yuan-pei

in Shanghai, 1933

Lu Hsun speaks to students of

the Peking Normal University, in 1932

Lu Hsun, Hsu Kuang-ping

and their little boy, Hai-ying, in 1933

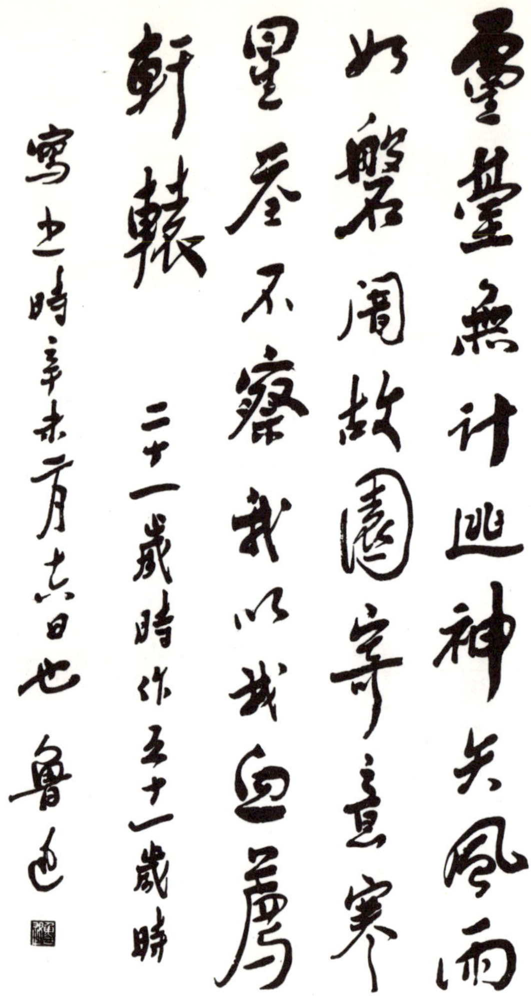

"Inscription on My Photo"

in the poet's own handwriting

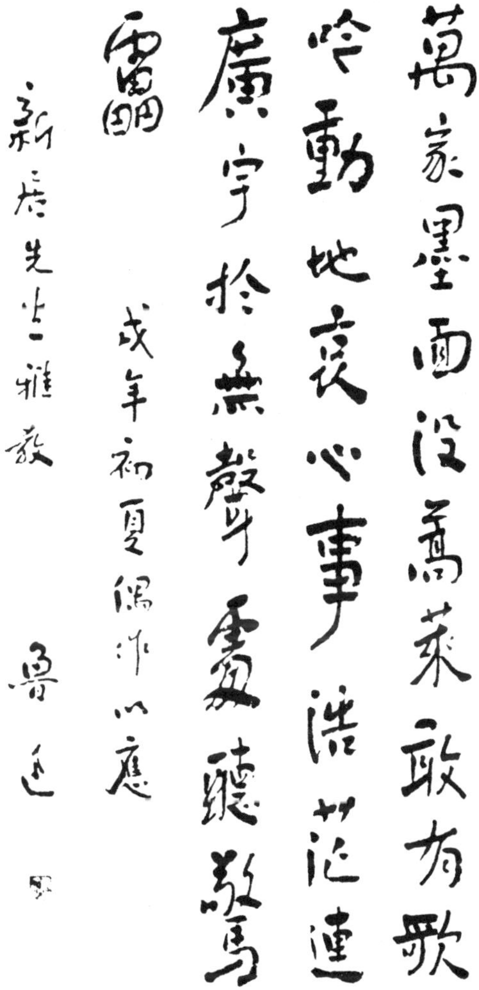

"An Untitled Poem (May 30, 1934)"

in the poet's own handwriting

Contents

(Poems in the Colloquial Style)

Acknowledgements

Since the publication of *Poems of Lu Hsun*, I have received letters and comments from home and abroad. This is a clear indication of people's love and deep concern for Lu Hsun, great Chinese writer of international importance.

This new edition is dedicated to the celebration of the centenary of Lu Hsun's birth. Printing errors are corrected through the joint efforts of the translator and the editorial board of the publisher, and the translations of some texts and notes have also been improved.

My special thanks should go to Dr. Barbara Findorff, secretary-general of the Europe China Association, Dr. Stephen S.N. Liu, poet and professor of Clark College, Nevada, Mr. N. Tyrrell from Oxford University, Professor Hsu Yuan-chong from Loyang Foreign Languages Institute, Professor Jon Kowallis from University of California, Berkeley, for their kind encouragement, invaluable suggestions and criticisms.

Huang Hsin-chyu

Spring 1981

Foreword

Forty years have elapsed since Lu Hsun, the great Chinese writer and founder of China's modern revolutionary literature, breathed his last. Today his brilliant writings still remain part of the most precious heritage of Chinese literature. Lu Hsun's poems both in the classical and colloquial styles only account for a small percentage of his writings, yet they are the component part of his whole literary achievements. This selection of Lu Hsun's poems may give a glimpse of Lu Hsun's mental development from a friend of the Chinese revolution to a great revolutionary writer.

No poets of Lu Hsun's contemporaries could ever be compared with him so far as the content and militancy of poetry are concerned. Who could mirror the deep sufferings of his times and shout battle cries for the broad toiling masses of China so forcefully and realistically as he did? Who could expose mercilessly the brutality and brazenness of the reactionary Kuomintang regime so sharply and point-blank as he did? It is Lu Hsun who presented the bright future to his people in deep water under the oppression of feudalism and imperialism. It is Lu Hsun who expressed his high esteem for the Chinese Communist Party headed by Mao Tse-tung before the dawn of China.

The poems of Lu Hsun shine with the brilliance of his wisdom and refinement, his strong sense of humour and his full poignancy of sarcasm. Every poem is a window into the character of Lu Hsun; each stanza is an insight into the reality of old China. Lu Hsun's poems written at different periods are either filled with the deep love for his motherland

and people or imbued with the revolutionary fire and militant spirit, which, to a certain extent, may reflect that he "was not only a great man of letters but also a great thinker and revolutionary." Lu Hsun did use his poems as a bugle call and battle cries of his times for his people.

However, it is a pity that no English edition of Lu Hsun's poems has been published since the birth of New China, though scattered English versions of his poems have appeared here and there, some even with errors or distortion of the originals. In view of this, the translator has made his first attempt at a systematic introduction of Lu Hsun's poems in English. As the visual and auditory effects of the original can hardly be in any way reproduced, it is almost impossible to find the exact equivalents in the English language to the tones, metres, feet and rhymes which contribute much to the musicality of the classical Chinese poetry. This is especially true with Lu Hsun's poems, because they were composed in the dark years under the reactionary Kuomintang rule. In order to avoid strict censorship, his poems were written in a rather restrained language and with a delicate touch of implications. This makes it more difficult for a Western mind to appreciate fully the associations implied in Lu Hsun's poems. For this reason the translator has made every conceivable effort to render the English version as easy to read as possible. In addition, he has also offered some explanatory notes in which the historical background of writing these poems is given for the convenience of the reader. Various notes and commentaries in the published works of Lu Hsun as well as reference notes and materials available have been consulted to ensure the reliability of the sources of information.

The translator has taken up this job not because he is well capable of cracking this hard nut, but because he is trying hard to do his bit in introducing something about this great writer and translator to the world. He would like to acknowledge his debts to Comrades Yeh Chun-chien, Ruth Weiss and many others from the Peking Foreign Languages Bureau, Peking Foreign Languages Press, as well as Professor Tsou Chiang from the Department of Foreign Languages at the Southwestern Teachers College, who is a poet and translator. They have kindly read the translation and notes with thorough scrutiny and made their valuable suggestions and warm encouragement throughout the repeated revisions of the manuscripts. Without their devoted help, it would be impossible to prepare this typescript for publication. The translator is looking forward to receiving further comments and criticisms for the improvement of his versions. Originally, this attempted work was meant for the fortieth anniversary of Lu Hsun's death on October 19, 1976. Since it was not ready for publication, it will be a great honour for him to dedicate this revision to the thirtieth anniversary of the founding of the People's Republic of China.

Huang Hsin-chyu

October 1, 1978

Poems of Lu Hsun
(In the Classical Style)

Inscription on My Photo

1903

There's no way for my heart to evade the arrows of Cupid[1],
While wind and rain like a millstone darken my homeland.[2]
Asking in vain the chilly stars to greet my people,
I'm resolved to shed my blood for my great motherland.

Translator's notes:

Lu Hsun wrote these lines on a photo which he sent to a friend[3] when he was studying in Japan. He had just cut off his queue which was a symbol of the feudal rule by the Ching dynasty (1644-1912). The aggression by the eight imperialist powers and the treacherous acts of the Ching government had thrown China into the abyss of semi-feudalism and semi-colonialism. The suffering of his country inspired Lu Hsun to the vow expressed in the last line of his poem. Lu Hsun remained true to his pledge throughout his life.

1. The "arrows of Cupid" here is used as a metaphor, hinting at the poet's deep love for his motherland.
2. Referring to feudalism and imperialism then dominating over the old China just like a millstone.
3. The friend here refers to Hsu Shou-shang (1883-1948), Chinese writer and professor, who was Lu Hsun's lifelong friend. He was the author of *The Lu Hsun I Knew*.

An Elegy on Fan Ai-nung[1]

July 22, 1912

1.

In these days buffeted by wind and rain,
How I cherish the memory of you, Fan Ai-nung!
Early streaked with grey is your thinning hair,
You glare at a snobbish toady with disdain.[2]
Things taste as bitter as sow-thistles in autumn,
Where is a proper place for an upright man?
Alas! Only after three months of separation,
Why a man so unyielding like you is gone forever?

2.

The riverside grass in your home town shines green,
For years you have roamed away in a foreign land.
Right after the foxes have just fled their den,[3]
On the stage those peach-wood puppets have shown.[4]
While your homeland is overcast with wild clouds,
Even the nights in dog-days seem to be cold and long!
Why drown yourself in the icy and clear cold waves,
Can they ever wash off your sorrows deep and strong?

3.

Taking up a cup of wine and commenting on our times,
You are always looking down upon those drunkards.
All men are drifting with the turbid currents,
But you have given up your life after a mere drink!
Our last farewell has separated us for ever and ever,
From now on never can I hear your revealing comments.
Since my old friends are swept away like clouds,
Now I'm living alone like dust, light as dust!

Translator's notes:

Lu Hsun wrote these lines to lament Mr. Fan Ai-nung, a friend of his. They two came from Shaohsing, Chekiang Province, and studied in Japan. In 1911, when Lu Hsun became principal of Shaohsing Normal School, Fan was appointed dean of studies. Dismissed by Lu Hsun's successor, Fan was out of work and lived a miserable life which led to his tragic death. Lu Hsun wrote these lines to express his deep condolences over this honest intellectual who had to commit suicide by drowning himself in a river in the dark days of old China.

1. Fan Ai-nung was a good friend of Lu Hsun. They got acquainted with each other while studying in Japan.
2. The snobbish toady refers to Ho Chi-chung, Fan Ai-nung's colleague. Ingratiating himself with Fu Li-chen, the new principal of the Shaohsing Normal School, Ho squeezed Fan out of his job. As Ho's given name Chi-chung has the same pronunciation as the Chinese for "chicken and insects", Lu Hsun here uses it as a pun to satirize Ho's preying upon people in lower positions. "Chicken and insects" was once used as a metaphor in Tu Fu's poem "Binding a Chicken", hinting at those who were preying upon one another. These poems on Fan Ai-nung were first published on August 21, 1919 in the *Minhsing Daily* published in Shaohsing under Lu Hsun's pen-name Huang Chi. In the postscript, we can find Lu Hsun's amusement with this pun which he referred to as an "extremely wonderful ironical masterstroke" ever used in his poetry writing.
3. Referring to the 1911 Revolution led by Dr. Sun Yat-sen who overthrew the feudal rulers of the Ching dynasty. "Foxes" here is used as a metaphor, hinting at the Ching rulers.
4. "Peach-wood puppets" refer to those feudal warlords such as Yuan Shih-kai who usurped the fruits of the 1911 Revolution.

To Uchiyama[1]

February 1931

For twenty years in Shanghai you have resided,
Every day you've witnessed something strange in China:
Those big shots seek no drugs to cure their ailments,
They resort to reading when they're getting bored.
Their countenance changes once they are in power,
And those beheaded are getting more and more,[2]
Of a sudden the bigwigs step down from the stage,[3]
Small wonder Amitabha[4] is chanted here and there!

Translator's notes:

Lu Hsun wrote these lines to expose the bloody slaughter of the revolutionaries and the deadly infighting among the Kuomintang warlords and politicians.

1. Uchiyama Kanzo (1885-1959) or Wu Chi-san (Chinese name offered jokingly by Lu Hsun) was a Japanese friend of the author. Uchiyama was the manager of a Japanese bookshop opened in Shanghai, which served as a shelter for Lu Hsun under the Kuomintang reign of terror.
2. Referring to Chiang Kai-shek's massacre of the Chinese Communists and the revolutionary masses on a large scale after he betrayed the revolution with his coup d'etat of April 12, 1927.
3. Referring to those warlords and politicians who were out of power.
4. "Amitabha" here is used as a pun, suggesting that those warlords and politicians chanted Buddhist sutras when they were thrown out of power. In certain Chinese dialects, "Amitabha" also means "Thank God!" , so the last line simply means that the common people would rejoice over the downfall of the warlords and politicians.

An Untitled Poem

February 1931

Used to spending the springtime in endless long nights[1] ,
I take refuge with my wife and kid, temples grey;
In dreams I dimly see my kind mother in tears,
The robbers'[2] flags keep changing over the city gates[3] .
What a torment to see my friends[4] become fresh ghosts!
Amid a forest of swords[5] I'm seeking for lines in wrath.
After chanting, I frown. Where can I put them down?[6]
And the icy moonlight shines over my black gown.

Translator's notes:

The Kuomintang police secretly arrested Jou Shih and other Left-wing writers on January 17, 1931, and Lu Hsun was also on the blacklist of the Kuomintang secret agents, so he had to take refuge with his wife and son in a Japanese hotel in Shanghai. In the dead of night on February 7, Jou Shih and twenty-three others were shot secretly at the Lunghua Garrison Headquarters in Shanghai. Lu Hsun wrote this poem to express his bitter indignation against the bloody massacre of the Chinese revolutionary writers by the Kuomintang police and his deep condolences over the revolutionary martyrs.

1. Referring to the dark days under the Kuomintang reign of terror.
2. Referring to the Kuomintang warlords.
3. Referring to Nanking, then capital of the Kuomintang central government.
4. Referring to Jou Shih and other revolutionary young writers murdered by the Kuomintang police.
5. "A forest of swords" is used as a metaphor, referring to the Kuomintang white terror.
6. This line implies that Lu Hsun found it hard to find a proper man or a proper place to voice his pent-up grief at a time like this.

To Mr. O.E.[1]
Going Back to Japan with Orchids

February 12, 1931

The pepper is burnt, the cassia plucked,[2]
and the noble-minded old,[3]
Only orchids grow alone in a secluded rock
and spread their pure fragrance.[4]
Why should I regret to spare these flowers
for my guest from far away?
Overgrown with thorns and brambles[5] , my homeland
is not yet awakened today!

Translator's notes:

This poem was written for a Japanese friend going back to Japan on February 12, 1931, five days after Jou Shih and other young revolutionary writers were murdered by the Kuomintang police. Under the bloody reign of terror, Lu Hsun wrote these lines with a mood of grief and pain.

1. O.E. stands for Obara Ejero, manager of a Japanese grocery in Tokyo selling Chinese orchids and other literary articles. Lu Hsun made friends with Obara Ejero through Uchiyama Kanzo.
2. In ancient China both trees were scented wood, here they are used as metaphors, hinting at the revolutionary youth being persecuted by the Kuomintang police.
3. Referring to Lu Hsun's friends who lost their militant will under the Kuomintang white terror.
4. This line refers to Lu Hsun's unyielding spirit of fighting alone bravely under the persecution of the Kuomintang reactionaries.
5. "Thornsand brambles" here are used as metaphors, hinting at the evil forces of old China.

To a Japanese Dramatic Critic

March 5, 1931

The beauty of the spring river remains as ever,
But homebound is today our overseas guest.
Do not glance back over this far-off stage,
Feng Shen[1] comes after *Pilgrimage to the West*![2]

Translator's notes:

Lu Hsun wrote this poem to a Japanese dramatic critic who had seen some fantastic and old plays in Shanghai at that time. In this poem, the author not only exposed the decadent art and literature in the Kuomintang-controlled areas but also lay bare the foul performance in the political arena of the Kuomintang reactionaries.

1. Referring to *Feng Shen Yen Yi* or *The Canonization Of The Gods,* a popular Ming dynasty (1386-1628) novel adapted to stage in Shanghai in the 1930's.
2. A popular classic Chinese novel by Wu Cheng-en (1500-1580) about taking back Buddhist scripture from India by Monk Triptika and his disciple, Monkey King's creating havoc in heaven. This novel was also adapted to stage in the early 1930's.

Song of the Hsiang Spirit[1]

March 5, 1931

Once the Hsiang River was said to be blue as dyed,
Now the Hsiang River is stained with the traces of blood.[2]
The Hsiang Spirit has dressed up and looks at the waters,
As the moon through the red clouds her white face shines.
Terror and silence reign over our land in the dead of night,[3]
The scented flowers wither, with no trace of spring.[4]
After playing her jasper lute, who would enjoy the tune?[5]
And the west gate is nothing but a scene of phoney peace.[6]

Translator's notes:

Lu Hsun wrote this poem to condemn the large-scale campaigns of "encirclement and suppression" launched by Chiang Kai-shek. The first half of this poem mirrors the massacre of the people and the second half depicts the reign of white terror in the Kuomintang-controlled areas. In this poem Lu Hsun denounced the towering crimes of the Kuomintang reactionaries and lamented the murdered Chinese people.

1. According to Chinese mythology, the Hsiang Spirit was the daughter of Emperor Yao, a wise ruler of ancient China, who married his daughter to another wise ruler, Emperor Shun, who succeeded Yao's throne. Later she was drowned in the Hsiang River and became the Goddess of the Hsiang. She was noted to be very beautiful and good at playing her jasper lute.
2. The Hsiang River is one of the largest rivers in Hunan Province. This line refers to the bloody massacre of the people by the Kuomintang reactionaries from 1927 to 1930 in Changsha, capital of Hunan Province.
3. This line refers to the two banks of the Hsiang River and other parts of the land under the reign of white terror.
4. This line refers to the desolate scene after the massacre.
5. This line refers to the sad tune of the Hsiang Spirit.
6. This line refers to Nanking and the Kuomintang-controlled areas where the Kuomintang chieftains could enjoy their "peaceful scene" while the common people went through deep sufferings.

An Untitled Poem

March 5, 1931

The great earth is under the shadow of sabres and swords,
And the boundless sky is ranked with clouds of war.
So few households are favoured with the spring breeze;[1]
Dead silence reigns over the expanse of the universe.[2]
Under heaven my homeland alone is in deep slumber,
And in midstream the joyful chanting is heard no more.[3]
Once my homeland is swept by wind and waves[4] ,
The trees and flowers[5] are then a scene of desolation!

Translator's notes:

This poem was written at a time when the first counter-revolutionary campaign of "encirclement and suppression" on the revolutionary red base areas launched by Chiang Kai-shek was crushed by the Chinese Red Army. Chiang Kai-shek attempted to launch his second campaign against the red base area. At the same time, he also launched his cultural "encirclement and suppression" against the Left-wing literary movement led by Lu Hsun. White terror reigned the entire land of old China. Lu Hsun indignantly denounced the towering crimes of the Kuomintang reactionaries in this poem.

1. This line simply means that in the dark days of old China, only the idle rich could enjoy a comfortable life.
2. Referring to the deplorable scene of old China.
3. This line implies that nobody could sing out the patriotic songs under the white terror.
4. Referring to Kuomintang's cultural "encirclement and suppression".
5. "Trees and flowers" are used as metaphors, hinting at the revolutionary writers. This line refers to the persecution of the Chinese revolutionary writers by the Chiang Kai-shek clique.

Two Untitled Poems

June 14, 1931

1

The mighty Yangtse flows eastward day and night,
A throng of heroes[1] are gathering to go abroad once more.
The Six Dynasties' glory[2] has become an old dream,
Only the crescent moon shines over the City of Rock[3].

2

Broken arms are buried beside the Rain Flower's Bed[4],
There're still some ripples left in the Worry-not Lake[5].
My dear ones I long to see are seen no more,
To the far-flung sky I sing a sad song for their sake!

Translator's notes:

Lu Hsun wrote these two poems for a Japanese couple. The first poem depicts the internal strife within the Kuomintang Central Government at Nanking. The author presents a dreary scene of the disintegrating Kuomintang regime, while the second one expresses his deep condolences over the murdered revolutionary martyrs.

1. "A throng of heroes" here refer to the Kuomintang warlords.
2. Referring to Wu, East Tsin, Sung, Chi, Liang and Chen dynasties from 3rd to 6th centuries, all with Nanking as capital.
3. Referring to the ancient name of the present-day Nanking.
4. Or Yu Hua Tai, the Hill of Raining Flowers where, according to Chinese legend, a Buddhist monk once preached so eloquently that the heavens rained flowers over this place. During the Kuomintang reign of terror, it was used as a secret execution ground to murder the Chinese patriots and revolutionaries. Now it is a historical site of Nanking.

5. Referring to Mo Tsou Lake, a well-known lake in Nanking, which was named after a beautiful Chinese sing-song girl during the Six Dynasties. This line implies that the lasting influence of the revolutionary martyrs will go down from generation to generation.

Seeing Mr. Masuda Wataru[1] off to Japan

December 2, 1931

Fine are the autumn tints on the island of Fursang[2],
The red maple-leaves shine bright in the gentle cold.
In breaking a willow twig[3] for my guest homebound,
I recall my youth[4] as my heart sails with the boat.

Translator's notes:

Lu Hsun wrote this poem to a Japanese friend in which he showed his friendship as well as the happy life of his youth in Japan when his heart was full of revolutionary fire.

1. Well-known Japanese sinologist, translator of Lu Hsun's *A Brief History of Chinese Fiction*. He was Lu Hsun's good friend and came to China to visit Lu Hsun for advice on his translation.
2. Or Land of Red Hibiscus, which is the ancient name of Japan.
3. In ancient China people used to break a willow twig to see off their friends.
4. Referring to Lu Hsun's recalling of his youth studying in Japan.

An Untitled Poem

January 23, 1932

Blood nourishes our Central Plain and the tough grass,[1]
The earth is frozen and brings forth flowers of spring[2] ;
Troubles often come to our "heroes", advisors fall ill,[3]
Tears shed over Sun Yat-sen's Tomb, dusk ravens cawing![4]

Translator's notes:

When Lu Hsun wrote this poem, the Chinese Red Army had won victories over Chiang Kai-shek's three campaigns of both military and cultural "encirclement and suppression", while the Kuomintang regime was beset with all sorts of contradictions and internal strife. In this poem, Lu Hsun sings praises of the revolutionary force led by the Chinese Communist Party as well as the rapid development of its red base areas. The author also satirizes the outwardly strong but inwardly weak Kuomintang reactionaries through this poem.

1. "Tough grass" refers to the revolutionary force. This line implies that the Kuomintang reactionaries can never put out the flames of revolution, on the contrary, the people will become stronger after the ordeal.
2. "Flowers of spring", symbolizing the revolutionary force.
3. "Heroes" here refer to the Kuomintang warlords; "advisors" refer to the Kuomintang politicians. In the latter half of 1931, there were civil wars between the Nanking and Kwangtung warlords. Chiang Kai-shek was forced to resign from presidency and Wang Ching-wei, vice-president of the Kuomintang Party, refused to attend its central party's sessions under the pretext of illness.
4. This line implies the deadly infighting among the Kuomintang politicians was so serious that Sun Ko, son of Dr. Sun Yat-sen, went to his father's tomb in the suburbs of Nanking and shed tears of sorrow. "Dusk ravens cawing", used as a metaphor, hinting at the Kuomintang's internal quarrels.

An Impromptu Poem

March 31, 1932

Where to go, since my writings are worth but a straw?[1]
It evokes my dreams to look far at the eastern clouds[2].
What I hate is the scented gardens[3], a desolate scene;
Spring orchids and autumn flowers each in its season![4]

Translator's notes:

When Lu Hsun wrote this poem, his house was reduced to ruins by the gunfire of the Sino-Japanese War in Shanghai. The author took refuge in Uchiyama's bookshop for a period of time. This impromptu poem shows Lu Hsun's love for his motherland and his deep hatred towards the Kuomintang reactionaries.

1. Referring to the persecution of revolutionary writers and their works under the dark rule of the Kuomintang.
2. "Eastern clouds" here refer to Japan. This line shows the poet was longing for his Japanese friends.
3. "Scented gardens" refer to the cultural fields, used as a metaphor, hinting at the Kuomintang's oppression and persecution of Chinese progressive culture and progressive writers.
4. "Spring orchids" refer to the young writers; "autumn flowers" refer to chrysanthemums. This line simply means that most of the young writers were murdered by the Kuomintang police, but Lu Hsun himself was left alone fighting bravely just like chrysanthemums braving the frost in autumn.

To Peng-tse[1]

March 31, 1932

All of a sudden a fairy[2] descends from the blue,
With her angel-like boys in two cloud-escorted rickshaws,[3]
Alas, Yao Peng-tse himself is not the son of Heaven[4] !
Our fairy has to run about exposed to hunger and cold.

Translator's notes:

Lu Hsun wrote this humorous poem at the request of Yao Peng-tse. In this poem Lu Hsun depicted the sufferings of the average Chinese intellectual during the Sino-Japanese War of 1932 in Shanghai.

1. Yao Peng-tse was Yao Wen-yuan's (one of the "Gang of Four") father. Yao Peng-tse was a Left-wing writer, but later he became a traitor. When Lu Hsun wrote this impromptu poem to Yao, he did not know Yao would betray the revolution in 1934. As soon as Yao became a traitor, Lu Hsun denounced him publicly.
2. The "fairy" here refers to Miss Mei Kung-teh humorously. Miss Mei was Mu Mo-tien's (another Left-wing writer who later became a traitor too) wife.
3. This line refers to the fact that Miss Mei Kung-teh took two rickshaws to find her husband, but failed to find him at Mr. Yao's.
4. "The son of Heaven" here refers to Emperor Mu, a god in Chinese mythology. It refers humorously to Mu Mo-tien, Miss Mei's husband, for Emperor Mu and Mr. Mu's names have the same pronunciation in Chinese!

Written after the January 28 Incident[1]

July 11, 1932

War clouds have dispersed, traces of spring remain,[2]
Both fine songs and the roar of guns are silent.[3]
I'm sorry to have no poem for my homebound friend,
But wish her a bon voyage from the depth of my heart.

Translator's notes:

This poem was written for a Japanese poetess who came to China in 1931 and kept correspondence with Lu Hsun for his advice on classical Chinese literature. When she went back to Japan, Lu Hsun wrote this poem to express their friendship.

1. Referring to the aggressive war in Shanghai launched by the Japanese imperialists on January 28, 1932.
2. This line refers to the fact that the Hongkou district of Shanghai where Lu Hsun lived was badly damaged by the Japanese bombings. Nothing but the last trace of spring remained. At that time Lu Hsun had to take shelter against the bombing raids at Uchiyama's bookshop in the British Settlement in Shanghai.
3. "Fine songs" here refer to the verses written by the Japanese poetess which could no longer be heard as she was leaving China for home. "Roar of guns" here refers to the cease-fire of the Shanghai War. When Lu Hsun returned to his home in Hongkou district after the cease-fire, he could not hear the roar of guns any more.

In Mockery of Myself

October 12, 1932

What can I ask for, since I have a spell of bad luck?
I've had my head knocked before I dare to turn over![1]
With a worn hat shading my face now I pass downtown,[2]
And in midstream I sail with some wine in a leaky boat.[3]
Fierce-browed, I coolly defy a thousand pointing fingers[4],
Head bowed, like a willing ox I serve the youngsters[5].
Well, hiding myself in this world of my small attic,
Why should I bother about the cycling of season[6]?

Translator's notes:

Lu Hsun wrote this poem to Liu Ya-tse (1887-1958), a Chinese poet and patriotic democrat. Under the reign of white terror, freedom of speech and of the press was suppressed, bookshops were smashed, Chinese patriots and progressives were arrested or murdered. Even Lu Hsun's name was on the blacklist of the Kuomintang agents. As Lu Hsun could not publish his works freely, he wrote this poem to express his ardent love for the broad masses and his deep hatred for the enemies of the people. As the title of this poem indicates, it is an irony and attack on the Kuomintang reactionaries.

1. This line refers to the author's being persecuted by the Kuomintang reactionaries.
2. This line refers to Lu Hsun's being shadowed by the Kuomintang agents.
3. This line implies that Lu Hsun's life was in jeopardy just like a leaky boat which might be wrecked at any time, yet he took it easy.
4. "A thousand pointing fingers" here refer to the attacks by Lu Hsun's enemies. This line simply means that Lu Hsun's unyielding spirit of waging tit-for-tat struggles against his enemies was so strong that he never gave up in face of enemy attacks.
5. The "youngsters" here is a metaphor, hinting at the broad toiling masses of the Chinese people. This line simply means Lu Hsun was willing to serve the people heart and soul.

6. "Cycling of seasons" here refers to the political climate of that time. This line implies that Lu Hsun was determined to wage uncompromising battles with the Kuomintang reactionaries no matter how dangerous the situation was.

Four Satirical Poems on Some Professors

1932-1933

1.

You've eaten your words by not shooting yourself,
So safe and sound you have passed forty![1]
Why not bet that fleshy head of yours
To boycott the teaching of dialectics?[2]
December 29, 1932

2.

What a pity for the Weaving Maid
To have become the wife of the "Horseherd"![3]
The magpies are too puzzled to find their way,[4]
For far, far away is the "Milk Way"[5] !
December 29, 1932

3.

There's such a kind of literature in the world,
About young ladies' plump hips it often talks![6]
When chicken soup is replaced by pork steaks,[7]
The Pei Hsin Bookshop is thus closed.[8]
1933

4.

A bigwig compiles a book of short stories,
Only a few are said to be up to standard.[9]
Though he may observe with a telescope,
It's pity he himself is short-sighted!
1933

Translator's notes:

These poems portrayed the ugly features of four professors in the 1930's. The first poem satirized Professor Chien Hsuan-tung, head of the Department of Chinese Language and Literature at the Peking Teachers University and editor of the *New Youth*. The second poem satirized Chao Ching-sen, professor of Futan University and editor of the Pei Hsin Bookshop in Shanghai. Once Chao mistranslated the Milky Way as "Niu-nai Lu", which in Chinese means literally a road built with milk — the Milk Way (while the correct Chinese term for the Milky Way should be "Yin-ho", the Silvery River). In the poem, Lu Hsun criticized his carefree attitude towards translation. The third poem satirized Chang Yi-ping, professor of the College of Arts at Chinan University, who was also editing the translation of world literature for the Pei Hsin Bookshop. Chang was notorious for his pornographic literature. The last poem satirized Professor Hsien Liu-yi.

1. Professor Chien once joked by saying that those who had passed forty should be shot. Lu Hsun satirized him for he was leading a comfortable life after forty! Chien was not so progressive as he was in the May 4th Movement.
2. Once Professor Chien was deadly against opening a course of dialectics for college students. He was stubborn enough to boycott the teaching of dialectics even if it meant his death.
3. These two lines refer to Chao Ching-sen's mistranslation of "Cowherd" into "Horseherd". The correct version should read "Cowherd", which was one of the Chinese zodiac constellations.
4. According to Chinese legend, the Cowherd and the Weaving Maid were two lovers who were separated by the Milky Way. On the seventh of July in the Chinese lunar calendar, they would enjoy their annual reunion when the magpies were supposed to bridge up the galaxy to make this reunion possible. Because of Chao's mistranslation, the kind-hearted magpies could never find a proper place to bridge up the galaxy!
5. " Milk Way " here refers to Professor Chao's another mistranslation. The correct version should read "Milky Way" instead of "Milk Way"! These two lines are simply humorous remarks on Chao's mistranslations. This also shows Lu Hsun's serious attitude towards translation.
6. Referring to Professor Chang Yi-ping's notorious pornographic literature.
7. Referring to Professor Chang's Yi-ping's editing of some children's best-sellers, so that he obviously profited from them to eat chicken broth to his heart's content.
8. The Pei Hsin Bookshop was first set up in Peking in 1924 and then moved to Shanghai. Later this bookshop was forced to close down for selling progressive books. When it was re-opened, it was involved in a lawsuit with the Chinese Islamic Society in 1933. Then the Pei Hsin Bookshop was closed down again because one of its publications insulted the Islams.
9. Professor Hsien Liu-yi compiled *A Collection of Model Short Stories* in which only the works of Lu Hsun, Mao Tun, Yeh Shao-chun, Hsieh Ping-hsin and Yuh Ta-fu were selected.

What I Have Heard

December 31, 1932

A mansion is opened in feasting with lanterns shining,
And a charming lass is dressed up to serve those drinking,
Recalling her dear departed beneath the scorched soil[1],
She tries to hide her tears by adjusting the silk stockings.

Translator's notes:

On the New Year's Eve of 1932, Lu Hsun wrote this poem for Mrs. Uchiyama. This poem expressed Lu Hsun's deep sympathy with those who were forced to serve the wine for the idle rich as well as his bitter indignation at those easy-going Kuomintang dissipated big shots for their gay bustle and debauchery. It portrayed vividly the sufferings of the people and condemned the crimes of the aggressive war.

1. The scorched soil here refers to the ruins after the war. This line recalls the victims after the War of January 28, 1932 in Shanghai launched by the Japanese aggressors.

Reply to Someone's Mockery

December 31, 1932[1]

Those heartless people may not be called real heroes,
Why are those with a tender love for their kids no true men?
Don't you know the fierce tiger roaring with the wind
Would cast back loving glances at its cub now and then?

Translator's notes:

This poem was composed in jest as a feedback to slanders that Lu Hsun had spoiled his only son, Chou Hai-ying. It was not published. In this poem Lu Hsun showed his great love and expectations for the younger generation.

1. According to a scroll on which was a signed, handwritten version of this poem, the date should be placed at somewhere between March 1931 and January 1932. Lu Hsun presented this scroll to a Japanese doctor who had cured dysentery for his son. However, there was no mention of Lu Hsun's writing this poem to a Japanese friend in 1931 in *Lu Hsun's Diary*. Instead, according to the Diary, it was on December 31, 1932 that the poem was sent to Lu Hsun's good friend, Yuh Ta-fu . In *A Supplement to A Collection of Uncollected Works* edited by Lu Hsun's wife Hsu Kuang-ping, she also put this poem in the period of 1932, hence the dating here.

Two Untitled Poems

December 31, 1932

1.

My native land is overcast with dark clouds,
And fine spring is kept away by the long night.
How can we bear any more sorrow on New Year's Eve?
Let's take some wine and globe-fish at the moment.

2.

A pretty girl with gleaming teeth sings a nice folk song,
It's late spring as the feast is over and guests are gone.
Somehow my old dreams have driven out the hangover,
I recall the cuckoo's call[1] in the shade by an oil lamp alone.

Translator's notes:

Lu Hsun wrote these two poems for two Japanese doctors respectively. The first poem expressed Lu Hsun's longing for China's liberation from the dark rule of the Kuomintang. The second poem showed his deep condolences over his friends who had been murdered by the Kuomintang reactionaries.

1. The "cuckoo's call" here is a metaphor, hinting at the murdered friends who have laid down their lives for China's freedom and independence.

An Untitled Poem

December 31, 1932

The sky seems higher as leaves fall on Lake Tungting[1] ,
And the blood of women has stained the army uniforms[2] .
Someone by the lake has to swallow up his chanting,[3]
For "Li Sao"[4] is lost amid the vast autumn waves.

Translator's notes:

Lu Hsun wrote this poem to expose the towering crimes of the massacre of the Chinese people during the fourth campaign of "encirclement and suppression" against the Hunan-Hupeh-Kiangsi revolutionary base area led by the Chinese Communist Party. It also denounced the crimes of Chiang Kai-shek's cultural "encirclement and suppression" against the Chinese revolutionary writers. This poem was written to Lu Hsun's friend Yuh Ta-fu to encourage the writers to write militant works.

1. Or the Tungting Lake, one of the largest lakes of China in Hunan Province.
2. Referring to the top-ranking officers of the Kuomintang. This line refers to the slaughter of the people and the debauchery of the Kuomintang brass hats.
3. This line implies that under the persecution of the Kuomintang reactionaries, it was not even possible to chant one's verses at the lakeside as the Chinese patriotic poet Chu Yuan (343-290 B.C.) did when he was banished by his king.
4. "Li Sao" or "Inviting Trouble" is the title of a long poem by Chu Yuan composed before his suicide. This long poem narrating his sorrows and disappointments in his exile is Chu Yuan's masterpiece. This line simply means that under the Kuomintang's reign of white terror there was neither freedom of speech nor freedom of writing.

New Year's Day, 1933

January 26, 1933

The clouds cap the lofty peaks and shelter the brass hats[1],
While the poor villagers are reduced to ashes by bombing[2].
After all, there's no better world than the concession,
Where spring comes anew in the sound of mahjong-playing!

Translator's notes:

Lu Hsun wrote this poem to present a striking contrast between the miserable life of the poor villagers who had to suffer from the Japanese wanton bombings and the easy and comfortable life of the idle rich who were living in the foreign settlement of Shanghai. It is indeed a strong accusation against the non-resistance of the Kuomintang reactionaries in face of the Japanese aggression.

1. The brass hats here refer to Chiang Kai-shek and company who took shelter on Mt. Lushan and had their headquarters set up there to conduct their non-resistant and anti-communist activities.
2. Referring to the bombing raids made by the Japanese bombers and the Kuomintang Air Force on the innocent Chinese civilians.

To a Japanese Painter

January 26, 1933

As bleak winds blow from Nanking, a myriad woods darken,[1]
All flowers have faded as fogs the blue sky are filling.[2]
I wish you could paint something new out of your creation,
May red hues be pervaded to tinge the hills of spring[3] !

Translator's notes:

Lu Hsun wrote this poem to a Japanese painter, Mochizuki Gyokusei, who visited China. The first half of this poem depicts the dark rule of the Kuomintang, and the latter half of this poem shows Lu Hsun's yearning for a bright future of the Chinese revolution. Through this poem, he encouraged the Japanese painter to see brightness through darkness and paint a new picture of bright spring hills.

1. This line implies the bloody massacre of the Chinese people by the Kuomintang reactionaries during the fourth campaign of "encirclement and suppression" carried out by Chiang Kai-shek.
2. This line refers to the dark rule of the Kuomintang.
3. "Hills of spring" is used as a metaphor, hinting at the bright future of the Chinese revolution.

Students and Jade Buddha

January 30, 1933

Nothing but a lonely deserted city here remains,
In such a hurry the curios are moved to the south.[1]
Those big shots used to boast quite a lot,[2]
They ask the "backbone"[3] to prop up their show just now.
Why blame the students for their panic fright?[4]
They have their reasons to seek safety in flight!
Alas, they're not lucky enough to be a jade Buddha[5],
As their humble lives are not even worth a cent!

Translator's notes:

Lu Hsun wrote this poem to satirize Chiang Kai-shek's non-resistant and capitulationist policy in face of the Japanese invasion of North China in 1933.

1. Referring to the evacuation of the curios from Peiping (present-day Peking) to Nanking in 1933. Chiang Kai-shek ordered the desertion of Peiping and let the Japanese invaders take this ancient city so easily.
2. This line satirizes Chiang Kai-shek and company only paid lip service to resisting the Japanese aggression but beat a retreat when the whole nation was threatened by the invasion.
3. "Backbone" here is an irony, referring to the college students used by the Kuomintang government. This line satirizes Kuomintang's persecution of the progressive students in deeds but only calling them "backbone" in words.
4. This line refers to the panic-stricken air of the young students when the Shanhai Pass (Pass of Seas and Mountains) fell into the hands of the Japanese aggressors on January 3, 1933. Since the Kuomintang top-ranking officials had fled from Peiping, why blame the students for their panic at such a critical moment?
5. "Jade Buddha" refers to the jade Buddha in Peiping which was made in jade with a height of four feet. This line is a poignant satire on the evacuation of the cultural relics such as the jade Buddha instead of the college students by the Kuomintang government.

Mourning the Fate of College Students

After Tsui Hao's Poem "Yellow Crane Tower"[1]

January 31, 1933

The rich and mighty have flown off with our "culture",[2]
Nothing but an empty city of culture[3] here remains.
The "culture", once gone from it, will never return,
This ancient city will be deserted for a thousand years.
Though special trains[4] line up at Chien Men Station,[5]
Unlucky and gloomy are those college students![6]
Where to resist, when the Japs have approached Yukuan?[7]
Still fooling around in the brothels are the brass hats!

Translator's notes:

Lu Hsun wrote this poem to satirize the Kuomintang government's removal of art treasures from Peiping and the refusal to evacuate the students when Peiping was threatened by the Japanese aggressor troops in 1933. This poem is a powerful exposure of Chiang Kai-shek's non-resistant and capitulationist policy in face of the Japanese invasion.

1. Tsui Hao (675-740), a Tang dynasty poet, once wrote a poem for the Yellow Crane Tower which is by the Yangtse west of Wuhan, Hupeh Province. The poem runs like this:
   An ancient man flew away on a yellow crane,
   Nothing but this empty tower here remains.
   The yellow crane, once gone, will never return.
   White clouds will float far away for a thousand years.
   O'er the river trees in Hanyang are all in sight,
   And on Parrot Island the lush and luxuriant grass.
   Where is my native place as the sun has set?
   The mist and waves o'er the river make me homesick!
2. "Culture" here refers to the art treasures to be moved to the south from Peiping by the Kuomintang high-ranking officials.
3. Referring to the ancient city of Peiping (present-day Peking).
4. Referring to the trains to evacuate high officials and the curios.

5. Referring to the old railway station of Peking.
6. This line refers to those college students who were refused evacuation by the Kuomintang government.
7. This line refers to the fall of the Shanhai Pass into the hands of the Japanese invaders on January 3, 1933.

Inscription of "Battle Cries"[1]

March 2, 1933

Doing literary work I'm caught in literary net,[2]
Rebelling against the world I've offended the world.[3]
Heaps of slanders might crush the bones of my kith and kin,
To what avail have I left my battle cries on the paper!

Translator's notes:

Lu Hsun wrote this poem as an inscription on his collection of short stories entitled *Battle Cries* to a Japanese friend who asked Lu Hsun to send him *Battle Cries* and *Wandering.*

1. Lu Hsun's earliest collection of short stories containing 14 stories (including one of Lu Hsun's masterpieces "The True Story of Ah Q" written between 1918-1922.
2. "Literary net" here is a metaphor, hinting at the persecution of Chinese revolutionary writers by the Kuomintang government.
3. This line refers to Lu Hsun's rebellion against the feudal rules and ideals of the old world, so he was under fierce attacks, slanders and abuses from his enemies.

Inscription on "Wandering"[1]

March 2, 1933

So desolate is the new garden of letters,[2]
And the old battlefront[3] is a scene of peace.
There remains one fighter between the two fronts,[4]
Still wandering alone shouldering his arms!

Translator's notes:

This poem was also written as an inscription on *Wandering* for a Japanese friend who asked Lu Hsun to send him this collection of short stories together with *Battle Cries.*

1. Lu Hsun's second collection of short stories written between 1924-1926.
2. Referring to the literary circles after the May Fourth Movement.
3. Referring to the old battlefield in Peiping where the anti-imperialist and anti-feudal new cultural movement was launched to wage fierce battles against the culture of feudalism in old China.
4. Referring to the two fronts between the new literary field and the old one.

A Lament for Yang Chuan[1]

June 21, 1933

How can I keep my soaring spirit of the old days?
I care nothing about the bloom or fall of flowers.
Never did I think to shed tears with the southern rain[2],
Weeping for my people's loss of another son so fine!

Translator's notes:

Lu Hsun wrote this poem right after attending Yang Chuan's funeral. To defend the people's rights and rescue imprisoned revolutionaries, Lu Hsun, Soong Ching Ling, Yang Chuan and others organized the China League for Civil Rights in June 1933, when a Kuomintang agent assassinated Yang, a fellow executive member of the League Committee and its secretary-general, Lu Hsun himself was also on the special agents' blacklist. Many people advised him to stay out of danger, nevertheless he went openly to the memorial meeting for Yang Chuan. Back from the meeting, he defiantly wrote this poem to express his unyielding revolutionary fighting spirit as well as his bitter indignation against the Kuomintang reactionaries.

1. Yang Chuan or Yang Hsing-fo was a native of Linchiang County, Kiangsi Province. He was a good friend of Lu Hsun. Unfortunately Yang was assassinated by the Kuomintang Blue Shirts (one of the secret agents' agencies) in Shanghai on June 18, 1933.
2. It was raining cats and dogs when Lu Hsun attended Yang Chuan's funeral. "Southern rain" here is used as a pun, implying that even the heavens were moved to tears. This line shows Lu Hsun's deep sorrow over the loss of a good comrade-in-arms.

An Inscription for San Yi Pagoda

June 21, 1933

San Yi Pagoda, where the remains of a Chinese dove from San Yi lane in Chaipei district, Shanghai, were buried, was built up jointly by some Japanese peasants.

Civilians were burnt to ashes in the flames of bombing,[1]
Nothing except a hungry dove survived by the broken walls.
A kind-hearted man chanced to deliver it from the sea of fire,
Only a pagoda was built up in Japan for its lasting memory.
The dove, if awakened, would carry stones as Ching Wei[2] did,
Let staunch fighters join hands to resist the adverse currents[3].
Tiding over this holocaust, brothers would still remain,
When we meet again, our smiles will sweep off our hatred!

A Japanese doctor[4] took a homeless dove back to Japan to feed after the Sino-Japanese War in Shanghai. The bird was quite all right at first, unfortunately it died at last. To bury the dove, a pagoda was built up. As I was asked to write a poem to mark this event, here I have rushed out a few lines to meet his kindness in one way or another.

Lu Hsun

June 21, 1933

Translator's notes:

Lu Hsun wrote this poem to mirror the resolution of the Chinese people to carry on the struggle against the aggressive war through to the end. In this poem Lu Hsun also expressed his friendly feeling towards the average Japanese people and his sincere hope that the Chinese people and the Japanese people would check the adverse currents shoulder to shoulder. Lu Hsun was far-sighted enough to predict a bright prospect of the Sino-Japanese friendship in this poem. His prediction had come true that a treaty of peace and friendship between China and Japan was finally concluded through the joint efforts of the peoples of these two countries.

1. This line refers to the wanton bombings by the Japanese bombers. During the Sino-Japanese War (January 28, 1932) in Shanghai, the San Yi lane in Chaipei district was reduced to ruins.
2. According to Chinese mythology, Ching Wei is a pheasant-like bird, which once carried stones at its beak to fill the East Sea. Here in this line it implies that the author wishes the Japanese workers and peasants would fill up the gap between the two peoples left over by the war.
3. "Adverse currents" here refer to the imperialist and fascist trends at that time.
4. A Japanese doctor here refers to Doctor Makoto Nishimula (1883-?), well-known Japanese biologist, who led a Japanese medical service team to Shanghai to support the Chinese people in February 1932.

An Untitled Poem

June 28, 1933

Our air-space is overclouded with winged generals[1],
Here in the snail-shelled hut a refugee remains.[2]
At night inviting his shadow from the puddle,[3]
He toasts with heaven's wine to the King's grace![4]

Translator's notes:

Lu Hsun wrote this poem to expose the towering crimes of the wanton bombings of the Japanese and Kuomintang Air Force on the Chinese peaceful civilians. This poem also showed Lu Hsun's deep concern over the sufferings of the common people.

1. "Winged generals" here refer to those Kuomintang Air Force officers who did not resist the Japanese aggression at that time but bombed the innocent Chinese civilians.
2. "Refugee" here refers to the survivor of the bombing raids. This line is a strong protest against the crimes of both the Japanese aggressors and the Kuomintang reactionaries.
3. This line simply means that under the bombing raids, nobody would come out at night, only the survivor's shadow would keep him company.
4. "Heaven's wine" here is an old euphemism for water, referring to the black water in the pool after raining. The whole line suggests a victim's sarcastic toast to an inhumane and dictatorial regime.

Two Poems for a Japanese Friend

August 21, 1933

1.

A limpid-eyed Kiangsu lass has dressed up in the morning,
She recalls her home town caressed by the lotus wind.
All new tunes have been offered, her lover's not seen,
And over the river the fire-like clouds are hanging!

2.

A Shensi lass plays her zither with a calm and serious air,
And the dust on the beam dances with the evening breeze.[1]
Suddenly the snow-white string is broken after the strain,
Lo, a star is shooting through the air with a whiz!

Translator's notes:

Lu Hsun wrote these two poems when a large part of China's land had fallen into the Japanese aggressors' hands, while the Kuomintang reactionaries suppressed the Chinese people. Droughts and floods threatened both north and south China, rendering the toiling masses of China homeless. A large number of refugees fled from the villages in this war-ravaged land and sing-song girls filled the streets of Shanghai and other big cities of China. These two poems give us an epitome of China's countryside under the imperialist aggression and the dark rule of the Kuomintang reactionaries. The first poem showed Lu Hsun's deep sympathy with the village girls' sufferings. The second poem expressed Lu Hsun's innermost feelings towards the crimes of the imperialists and the Kuomintang reactionaries. It also revealed the revolutionary strength hidden in the hearts of the Chinese people.

1. This line implies that even the dust on the beam was moved to dance with the nice music played by the girl.

An Untitled Poem

November 27, 1933

On a pretty lotus bloom rests peacefully the Hsiang Spirit,[1]
The orchids over the fields give comfort to the clear-headed.[2]
Alas, the wide fields are overgrown with evil weeds at last![3]
Even living in exile the banished[4] will spread the fragrance.

Translator's notes:

Lu Hsun wrote this poem to a Japanese bard. When he wrote this poem, old China was under the reign of white terror. This poem encouraged the revolutionary workers of literature and art to stick it out in the fight against the Kuomintang reactionaries and work still harder for spreading Marxism under terrible conditions.

1. "A pretty lotus bloom" here refers to the proletarian revolutionary literature and art. "The Hsiang Spirit" here is used as a metaphor, hinting at the people led by the Chinese Communist Party.
2. "The clear-headed" here implies the Chinese revolutionary cultural workers, while the "orchids" here implies the heroic Red Army men and the people in the revolutionary base areas under the leadership of the Chinese Communist Party. This line simply means that the revolutionary cultural workers were greatly inspired by the victories won by the Red Army.
3. "Evil weeds" here refer to the special agents and lackeys of the Kuomintang government.
4. The "banished" here refers to those who were hunted and persecuted by the special agents and running dogs of the Kuomintang reactionaries.

Advise Yuh Ta-fu Not to Move His Family to Hangchow

December 30, 1933

King Chien passed away long ago, yet his spectre remains,[1]
Premier Wu was gone with the waves without leaving a trace.[2]
The woods warm with sunshine are haunted by the falcons,[3]
Those hills perfumed with flowers are shaded by mountains.[4]
How bleak and bare is the Tomb of General Yueh Fei[5]!
What a dreary scene is Hermit Lin Fu's crane grove![6]
Why not move your family to a farther and wider place?
It's spacious enough for chanting, braving the storms!

Translator's notes:

Lu Hsun wrote this poem to Wang Yen-hsia, wife of Yuh Ta-fu (1896-1945), a novelist, one of the chief members of the Creation Society (a well-known literary association set up in 1921 and banned by the Kuomintang government in February 1929) was then wanted by the Kuomintang agents. That's why he wanted to move his family from Shanghai to Hangchow. Seeing that Hangchow was then a reactionary stronghold of the Kuomintang reactionaries, Lu Hsun wrote this poem to prevent Yuh from doing so. Lu Hsun encouraged Yuh to steel himself through revolutionary storms by giving up his illusions towards the high officials of the Kuomintang government.

1. King Chien refers to Chien Liu, the King of the Wu Yueh Kingdom during the Five Dynasties (907-960), who was noted for his cruelty in fleecing his people. This line implies that there were other "King Chiens" among the Kuomintang rulers in Hangchow.
2. Premier Wu refers to Prime Minister Wu Tzu-hsu who was loyal to the King of Wu, who killed this loyal prime minister and threw his remains into a river. This line implies that Yuh would fall a victim under the high-handed policy of

the Kuomintang authorities if he did want to move his family and stay in Hangchow.

3. This line implies the danger of being harmed by the Kuomintang agents fierce as the falcons.
4. This line advises Yuh not to be charmed by the nice scenery of Hangchow.
5. General Yueh Fei was a famous general in the Sung dynasty who resisted the Tartars and was finally murdered by an evil minister Chin Hui. Near the West Lake, there was Yueh Fei's tomb.
6. Hermit Lin Fu was a Sung poet (967-1028), who was a hermit in the Northern Sung dynasty. Lin had his cottage at the Solitary Hill near the West Lake of Hangchow, where he reared cranes and planted plum trees to enjoy his retiring life.

An Untitled Poem

December 30, 1933

War and floods are nothing new in our land,
In the desolate village remains but a fisherman.
When he wakes up from his dream in the dead of night,
Where is the place to find him a decent living?

Translator's notes:

Lu Hsun wrote this poem to Huang Cheng-chiu, a young woman editor of *Modern Woman*, who asked Lu Hsun to write something for the magazine. In this poem Lu Hsun condemned the crimes of the Kuomintang government in waging civil wars against the Chinese people. This poem was also an accusation against the cruel oppression of the people by the Kuomintang reactionaries.

Written Jokingly after Reading the Fabricated News about My Suffering from "Meningitis"

March 16, 1934

How can the fierce-brows[1] vie with the moth-brows[2] ?
Little did I think to have offended those fair ladies[3] !
Nowadays they even curse me in such a queer way,[4]
But this poor brain of mine remains as cold as ice![5]

Translator's notes:

Lu Hsun wrote this poem to refute those who fabricated the news about Lu Hsun's suffering from meningitis. In this poem we may see the author's humour and his poignant sarcasm.

1. Referring to Lu Hsun himself who was throwing his contemptuous glare at the rumour-mongers.
2. "Moth-brows" orginally refer to the ancient beauties of Chinese women, here they refer to those who used to spread rumours about Lu Hsun to please their masters.
3. "Fair ladies" here refer to those Kuomintang writers.
4. This line refers to those who were trying hard to undermine the prestige of Lu Hsun and informed against him. When they failed to reach their mean purpose, they went so far as to fabricate news against Lu Hsun.
5. This line simply means that Lu Hsun was easy and calm in face of all sorts of slanders and frame-ups by his enemy.

An Untitled Poem

May 30, 1934

A host of gloomy faces are amid the brambles,[1]
Who has the guts to sing out the earth-shaking sorrows?[2]
Ah, my heart is closely linked with the vast world,[3]
And I can hear the roar of thunder in this dead silence![4]

Translator's notes:

Lu Hsun wrote this poem in China's darkest years – darkness before dawn. On October 7, 1961, Chairman Mao Tse-tung copied out this poem and presented it to some Japanese friends visiting China to encourage the Japanese people resolutely engaged in revolutionary struggles. This is not only an inspiration to the Japanese people but also an encouragement to the oppressed peoples around the world.

When Lu Hsun wrote this poem, Chiang Kai-shek was concentrating one million troops to launch his fifth campaign of "encirclement and suppression" against the revolutionary base area. The Japanese invaders also stepped up their aggression by attacking North China. As a result, the Chinese people underwent untold sufferings. During those darkest years, Lu Hsun was not in the least wavering or compromising with the Kuomintang reactionaries. His firm belief was that the bloody slaughter and cruel oppression of the people would only lead to the people's dauntless resistance, and the storm of the Chinese revolution would shake the old world!

1. Referring to those undernourished people suffering from hunger and cold and those perished amid the brambles.
2. This line presents a true picture of the harsh reality under the dark rule of the Kuomintang. Countless families were reduced to homeless, but they could only swallow up their tears and buried their hatred in their hearts.
3. This line shows Lu Hsun's deep concern for the Chinese revolution led by Chairman Mao and the Communist Party of China.

4. "The roar of thunder" suggests the militant battle cries of the people and the storm of the Chinese revolution."Dead silence" implies the superficial silence under the KMT reign of terror. This line shows the firm belief that the victory of the revolution would come soon and the dark rule of the Kuomintang is bound to come to an end.

Thoughts on an Autumn Night

September 29, 1934

The time is fooled away behind the silk curtains,[1]
Buddhist services are held near the execution ground.[2]
The cuckoo's call has turned the green grass brown,[3]
And the weeds thick with thorns the fields adorn.[4]
Whence come the cakes and fruits to a thousand Buddhas?[5]
What a wonderful show to have invited these stars![6]
The cock crows at midnight in chorus with wind and rain,[7]
To feel the cool fresh air I sit up and light a cigar.[8]

Translator's notes:

This poem is flooded with implications. Lu Hsun wrote this poem because he was deeply stirred by the Kuomintang's dark rule. Obviously this poem was a stark exposure of the cultural "encirclement and suppression" by the Kuomintang reactionaries. It is a powerful accusation against their crimes and hypocrisies.

1. This line refers to the shameless and dissipated life of the Kuomintang big shots.
2. This line exposed the hypocrisy of the Kuomintang government. While holding Buddhist services, they were slaughtering the Chinese people.
3. This line implies the destruction of Chinese culture by the Kuomintang reactionaries.
4. This line implies the desolate scene of the literary field with only the militant works by Lu Hsun and his comrades-in-arms to carry on the fight against the enemy.
5. "Cakes and fruits" implies the literary works, "a thousand Buddhas" implies the reactionary rulers. This line implies that it was impossible for those men of letters hired by the Kuomintang government to write out good pieces to serve their masters.
6. This line refers to the fact that some of the well-known stage and film stars were invited to give performances at the Buddhist service held in Hangchow on April 28, 1934.

7. "Cock crows" implies the dawn of China, "wind and rain" implies the deep sufferings of the Chinese people in old China.
8. This line implies the author was ready to greet the advent of dawn, showing his dauntless spirit of waging new battles with his eloquent pen.

To Hsu Kuang-ping[1]

An Inscription on "Chiehtzuyuan's Guide to Traditional Chinese Paintings Vol. 111"[2]

December 9, 1934

For ten years, hand in hand we've gone through thick and thin,[3]
Like two fish out of water, we've each other sadly moistened;[4]
Let's try to feast our tired eyes on these paintings,
Only our own hearts can feel the joys and sorrows therein.

Translator's notes:

Lu Hsun wrote this poem to his wife on a book of paintings with his own inscription on it to encourage each other for newer and harder battles against the Kuomintang reactionaries. This short poem shows their militant friendship during the hard times they have gone through.

1. Lu Hsun's wife.
2. This album in three volumes entitled *Mustard Seeds Garden Manual of Painting* (1679-1701) was published in the early days of the Ching dynasty (1644-1912).
3. Referring to the years from 1925 to 1934 during which Lu Hsun and his wife were fighting shoulder to shoulder and had undergone untold sufferings and hardships.
4. "Like two fish out of water" here is used as a metaphor, hinting at their sharing each other's weal and woe under the reign of white terror during the reactionary Kuomintang rule.

An Impromptu Poem
Composed at Late Autumn

October 1935

Shocked to learn the chill of autumn has swept the land,[1]
How can I reveal the warmth of spring through my pen?
Mingled feelings have sunk into the vast sea of men,[2]
All officials took flight in the sighing autumn wind.[3]
To this bleak lake naked of reeds a grey beard I return,[4]
I shudder with cold to fall from the clouds in my dream.
Trying hard to listen for the cock-crows, but in vain,[5]
I get up only to find the Dipper near the horizon![6]

Translator's notes:

This is Lu Hsun's last poem before his death. When Lu Hsun wrote this poem, the Chinese Red Army led by Chairman Mao and Chu Teh had began the world-famous Long March. In October, 1935 the Red Army reached North Shensi triumphantly. This brought hopes to the Chinese people who were in deep water under the heels of the Japanese aggressors and the dark rule of the Kuomintang. In this poem Lu Hsun condemned the crimes of Chiang Kai-shek's capitulationist policy with bitter indignation. At the same time, Lu Hsun expressed his firm belief in the sure victory of the Chinese revolution led by the Chinese Communist Party headed by Chairman Mao Tse-tung.

1. This line refers to the national crisis in the first half of 1930's when China was threatened by the Japanese aggression as well as the dark rule of the Kuomintang.
2. This line implies the bitter feeling Lu Hsun had when he could not voice his anger under the white terror, especially the Chinese nation's existence was hung in the balance.
3. Referring to Lu Hsun's indignation against the panic-stricken Kuomintang top-ranking officials' flight to the south in face of the Japanese aggression in

1935.

4. This line implies the miserable plight of the broad toiling masses under the reactionary Kuomintang rule.
5. This line implies Lu Hsun's longing for daybreak.
6. This line implies the advent of dawn, suggesting that the final victory of the Chinese revolution will come soon.

Poems of Lu Hsun
(In the Colloquial Style)

Why I Lost My Love

(after Chang Heng's Poem[1] in a New Trivial Rhyme)

October 3, 1924

My love lives on the slope of a hill,
I'm trying to have a date with her,
But the hill is a bit too high,
It can't be helped, with my head down,
My gown is wet with tears.
My love presents me with a handkerchief,
It is embroidered with a hundred butterflies;
What should I send her in return?
Nothing more than an owl I can offer!
Since then our romance has come to an end,
I know not why I'm shivering with fright!

My love lives in a noisy town,
I'm trying to have a date with her,
But it's a bit too crowded.
It can't be helped, with my head up,
My ears are wet with tears.
My love presents me with a picture of twain swallows;
What should I send her in return?
Nothing more than some ice-frozen sweetmeats I can offer!
Since then our romance has come to an end,
I know not why I am at a loss!

My love lives by a riverside,
I'm trying to have a date with her,
But the water in the river is too deep,
It can't be helped, cocking my head,

The edge of my gown is wet with tears.
My love presents me with a gold watch-band;
What should I send her in return?
Nothing more than some aspirin I can offer!
Since then our romance has come to an end,
I know not why I've got a nervous breakdown!

My love lives in a family rich and mighty;
I'm trying to have a date with her,
But where can I get a car to ride?
It can't be helped, shaking my head,
My tears are trickling down like a stream.
My love presents me with some roses;
What should I send her in return?
Nothing but a coral snake!
Since then our romance has come to an end,
I know not why — just let her get away!

Translator's notes:

Lu Hsun wrote this trivial rhyme to satirize the poems about romance prevalent at that time. This poem was a poignant satire on the bourgeois view-point of love: "Love is everything" and "Fall in love at first sight", etc.

1. Chang Heng was a noted Chinese scientist and man of letters in the Eastern Han dynasty (25-220) who invented the first seismograph. Once Chang Heng wrote a poem of romance entitled "My Four Worries about My Love". Lu Hsun wrote this poem after Chang's rhyme.

Inscription on "Nothing More"[1]

For the last six months,
I have seen lots of blood and tears[2],
Yet I can have nothing
More than some random thoughts.
The tears are wiped off,
The bloodstains have faded;
But those murderers with steel swords[3]
Or with soft blades[4] remain at large.
Yet I can have nothing
More than some "random thoughts".
When the "random thoughts"
Are even "placed to where they should be"[5],
I can have nothing but "NOTHING MORE"!

P.S. The above lines were written on the night of October 14, 1926 as the epilogue for my collection of random thoughts of that year. I now have them taken as an inscription for the collection of random thoughts of 1927.

Lu Hsun

October 30, 1928

Translator's notes:

Lu Hsun wrote this poem in colloquial Chinese when he completed revising *A Sequel to Bad Luck* as a postscript. He used this poem once more as an inscription on his *Nothing More.* In this poem, Lu Hsun condemned Tuan Chi-jui and his warlord government who used his "steel swords" and the reactionary writers who used their pens as their "soft blades" to murder the Chinese patriots and the revolutionary masses. After April 12, 1927, Chiang Kai-shek betrayed the revolution with his coup d'etat by massacring the Chinese Communists and progressives. Lu Hsun used this poem as an inscription for his collection of essays to denounce the towering crimes of Chiang Kai-shek.

1. A collection of twenty-nine essays written in 1927 and one in 1926 by Lu Hsun.
2. Referring to the murder of Chinese patriots by the northern warlords.
3. In March 1926, the Japanese imperialists, allied with those of Britain and the United States , started an armed intervention in China which aroused great indignation. A demonstration in protest took place. On March 16, 1926, Tuan Chi-jui, head of a northern warlord government, ordered his guards with rifles and swords to surround and slaughter hundreds of young people who had come unarmed to Government House for the demonstration against his sell-out of China to the imperialists.
4. Referring to Chen Hsi-yung, the lackey of the warlord government, and his like who tried to find excuses for the brutal slaughter of Chinese students by the warlord government of Tuan Chi-jui.
5. This is quoted from Chen Hsi-yuan's correspondence with Hsu Chih-mo in which Chen attacked Lu Hsun.

Song of the Good Sort

December 11, 1931 (published)

All day long meetings are held in the south,
Smoke of war swirls up all at once in the north.[1]
The southerners yell and the northerners flee,
All cables and petitions keep pouring in.[2]
And the bigwigs abuse one another in turn,
Each of them tries to claim to be sweet as honey.
Officials mock at Chiang's double-dealing,[3]
Officers accuse their opponents of being cunning.[4]
Amid their abuses our fair land is lost!
Amid their abuses the people are levied more taxes!
Since the land is lost and more taxes are levied,
The yellings and abuses have simmered down at last.
Then officials are suffering from tooth-aches,
And generals are heading for the hot springs.
Now it's clear that no one was a traitor,
Why not write off the past misunderstandings?
Since each and everyone is a good sort now,
Let's get together and smoke a nice cigar!

Translator's notes:

Lu Hsun wrote this lampoon to ridicule the reactionary politicians and warlords within the two factions of the Kuomintang when the Japanese occupied northeast China on September 18, 1931. The title is an ironic one, suggesting the opposite meaning of a good sort.

1. This line refers to the Japanese invasion of Chinchow in the northeast on November 22, 1931.
2. This line refers to the fact that patriotic students all over China went to the

Kuomintang central government in Nanking to appeal to Chiang Kai-shek for resisting the Japanese aggression.

3. This refers to Chiang Kai-shek who claimed to be following the example of the patriotic general Yueh Fei (1103-1142) who resisted the Tartars.
4. This refers to Chiang Kai-shek's opponents headed by Wang Ching-wei in Canton. The supporters of Chiang here compared them to the treacherous Chin Hui (1090-1155), an evil prime minister in the Sung dynasty who murdered Yueh Fei and sued for peace with the Tartars.

A Nanking Ballad

December 25, 1931

All bigwigs[1] swear in before Sun Yat-sen's Tomb,
While robbers[2] are passing themselves off as saints.
They stand in silent tribute for ten minutes[3],
In fact for the art of boxing[4] each racks his brains!

Translator's notes:

This is a political satire written in the new style. Lu Hsun wrote this poem to satirize the ugly features of the Kuomintang Party bosses. In this poem Lu Hsun artfully displays his humour and sarcasm.

1. "Bigwigs" here refer to the Kuomintang chieftains such as Chiang Kai-shek, Wang Ching-wei, Lin Sen and Sun Ko, son of Dr. Sun Yat-sen, etc. "Swear in" here refers to the fact that in October 1931, Chiang Kai-shek was forced to resign from presidency. Lin Sen was then made the new president. They decided to swear in before Sun Yat-sen's mausoleum in the suburbs of Nanking.
2. "Robbers" here refer to the Kuomintang bosses who fleeced the Chinese toiling masses just like robbers.
3. This line refers to the Kuomintang's routine service of having three minutes' silence for the late Dr. Sun Yat-sen, founder of the Kuomintang Party, at the beginning of each meeting to show their loyalty to Sun Yat-sen. Here ten minutes is an exaggeration to satirize the hypocrisy of the Kuomintang Party bosses.
4. "Art of boxing" here is a sarcastic remark, suggesting that each of the Kuomintang bosses was trying hard to find out ways and means to topple down his opponents even when he stood in silent tribute before Sun Yat-sun's tomb.

Addendum:

A Lament for Miss Ting[1]

June 28, 1933

High towers are choked with breathless pitch-dark night,[2]
The willow-cutting spring wind brings a bleak autumn sight.
Plaintive tunes are hushed, as jasper lute lays dust-laden,[3]
Alas, our homeland is deserted with no more lady so fine!

Translator's notes:

On May 14, 1933, Miss Ting was kidnapped in Shanghai by the Kuomintang agents. Meanwhile, it was rumoured that she was murdered in Nanking. Lu Hsun wrote this poem to voice his sorrow.

1. Miss Ting here refers to Ting Ling, noted Chinese woman writer.
2. This line presents a dreary scene of the white terror under the Kuomintang rule.
3. This line refers to the ban of revolutionary writings and the persecution of Chinese writers by the Kuomintang government.

Appendix

Chinese Originals of the Poems

Inscription on My Photo

自题小像

一九〇三年

灵台无计逃神矢，风雨如磐黯故园。
寄意寒星荃不察，我以我血荐轩辕。

An Elegy on Fan Ai-nung

哀范君三章

一九一二年七月二十二日

一
风雨飘摇日，余怀范爱农。
华颠萎寥落，白眼看鸡虫。
世味秋荼苦，人间直道穷。
奈何三月别，竟尔失畸躬！

二
海草国门碧，多年老异乡。
狐狸方去穴，桃偶已登场。
故里寒云恶，炎天凛夜长。
独沉清冷水，能否涤愁肠？

三

把酒论当世，先生小酒人。
大圜犹茗艼，微醉自沉沦。
此别成终古，从兹绝绪言。
故人云散尽，我亦等轻尘！

To Uchiyama

赠邬其山

一九三一年二月

廿年居上海，每日见中华：
有病不求药，无聊才读书。
一阔脸就变，所砍头渐多。
忽而又下野，南无阿弥陀。

An Untitled Poem

无　题

一九三一年二月

惯于长夜过春时，挈妇将雏鬓有丝。
梦里依稀慈母泪，城头变幻大王旗。
忍看朋辈成新鬼，怒向刀丛觅小诗。
吟罢低眉无写处，月光如水照缁衣。

To Mr. O.E. Going Back to Japan with Orchids

送O. E. 君携兰归国

一九三一年二月十二日

椒焚桂折佳人老，独托幽岩展素心。
岂惜芳馨遗远者，故乡如醉有荆榛。

To a Japanese Dramatic Critic

赠日本歌人

一九三一年三月五日

春江好景依然在，远国征人此际行。
莫向遥天望歌舞，西游演了是封神。

Song of the Hsiang Spirit

湘灵歌

一九三一年三月五日

昔闻湘水碧如染，今闻湘水胭脂痕。
湘灵妆成照湘水，皎如皓月窥彤云。
高丘寂寞竦中夜，芳荃零落无余春。
鼓完瑶瑟人不闻，太平成象盈秋门。

An Untitled Poem

无　题

一九三一年三月五日

大野多钩棘，长天列战云。
几家春袅袅，万籁静愔愔。
下土惟秦醉，中流辍越吟。
风波一浩荡，花树已萧森。

Two Untitled Poems

无题二首

一九三一年六月十四日

一

大江日夜向东流，聚义群雄又远游。
六代绮罗成旧梦，石头城上月如钩。

二

雨花台边埋断戟，莫愁湖里余微波。
所思美人不可见，归忆江天发浩歌。

Seeing Mr. Masuda Wataru off to Japan

送增田涉君归国

一九三一年十二月二日

扶桑正是秋光好，枫叶如丹照嫩寒。
却折垂杨送归客，心随东棹忆华年。

An Untitled Poem

无　题

一九三二年一月二十三日

血沃中原肥劲草，寒凝大地发春华。
英雄多故谋夫病，泪洒崇陵噪暮鸦。

An Impromptu Poem

偶　成

一九三二年三月三十一日

文章如土欲何之，翘首东云惹梦思。
所恨芳林寥落甚，春兰秋菊不同时。

To Peng-tse

赠蓬子

一九三二年三月三十一日

蓦地飞仙降碧空，云车双辆挈灵童。
可怜蓬子非天子，逃去逃来吸北风。

Written after the January 28 Incident

一二八战后作

一九三二年七月十一日

战云暂敛残春在，重炮清歌两寂然。
我亦无诗送归棹，但从心底祝平安。

In Mockery of Myself

自　嘲

一九三二年十月十二日

运交华盖欲何求，未敢翻身已碰头。
破帽遮颜过闹市，漏船载酒泛中流。
横眉冷对千夫指，俯首甘为孺子牛。

躲进小楼成一统，管他冬夏与春秋。

Four Satirical Poems on Some Professors

教授杂咏四首

一

作法不自毙，悠然过四十。
何妨赌肥头，抵当辩证法。
（一九三二年十二月二十九日）

二

可怜织女星，化为马郎妇。
乌鹊疑不来，迢迢牛奶路。
（一九三二年十二月二十九日）

三

世界有文学，少女多丰臀。
鸡汤代猪肉，北新遂掩门。
（一九三三年）

四

名人选小说，入线云有限。
虽有望远镜，无奈近视眼。
（一九三三年）

What I Have Heard

所　闻

一九三二年十二月三十一日

华灯照宴敞豪门，娇女严装侍玉樽。
忽忆情亲焦土下，佯看罗袜掩啼痕。

Reply to Someone's Mockery

答客诮

一九三二年十二月三十一日

无情未必真豪杰，怜子如何不丈夫。
知否兴风狂啸者，回眸时看小於菟。

Two Untitled Poems

无题二首

一九三二年十二月三十一日

一

故乡黯黯锁玄云，遥夜迢迢隔上春。
岁暮何堪再惆怅，且持卮酒食河豚。

二

皓齿吴娃唱柳枝，酒阑人静暮春时。
无端旧梦驱残醉，独对灯阴忆子规。

An Untitled Poem

无　题

一九三二年十二月三十一日

洞庭木落楚天高，眉黛猩红涴战袍。
泽畔有人吟不得，秋波渺渺失离骚。

New Year's Day, 1933

二十二年元旦

一九三三年一月二十六日

云封高岫护将军，霆击寒村灭下民。
到底不如租界好，打牌声里又新春。

To a Japanese Painter

赠画师

一九三三年一月二十六日

风生白下千林暗，雾塞苍天百卉殚。
愿乞画家新意匠，只研朱墨作春山。

Students and Jade Buddha

学生和玉佛

一九三三年一月三十日

寂寞空城在，仓皇古董迁。
头儿夸大口，面子靠中坚。
惊扰讵云妄？奔逃只自怜：
所嗟非玉佛，不值一文钱。

Mourning the Fate of College Students

吊大学生

一九三三年一月三十一日

阔人已骑文化去，此地空余文化城。

文化一去不复返，古城千载冷清清。
专车队队前门站，晦气重重大学生。
日薄榆关何处抗，烟花场上没人惊。

Inscription on "Battle Cries"

题《呐喊》

一九三三年三月二日

弄文罹文网，抗世违世情。
积毁可销骨，空留纸上声。

Inscription on "Wandering"

题《彷徨》

一九三三年三月二日

寂寞新文苑，平安旧战场。
两间余一卒，荷戟独彷徨。

A Lament for Yang Chuan

悼杨铨

一九三三年六月二十一日

岂有豪情似旧时，花开花落两由之。
何期泪洒江南雨，又为斯民哭健儿。

An Inscription for San Yi Pagoda

题三义塔

一九三三年六月二十一日

三义塔者，中国上海闸北三义里遗鸠埋骨之塔也，在日本，农人共建之。

奔霆飞熛歼人子，败井颓垣剩饿鸠。
偶值大心离火宅，终遗高塔念瀛洲。
精禽梦觉仍衔石，斗士诚坚共抗流。
度尽劫波兄弟在，相逢一笑泯恩仇。

西村博士于上海战后得丧家之鸠，持归养之；初亦相安，而终化去。建塔以藏，且征题咏，率成一律，聊答遐情云尔。一九三三年六月二十一日鲁迅并记。

An Untitled Poem

无　题

一九三三年六月二十八日

禹域多飞将，蜗庐剩逸民。
夜邀潭底影，玄酒颂皇仁。

Two Poems for a Japanese Friend

赠人二首

一九三三年八月二十一日

一

明眸越女罢晨装，荇水荷风是旧乡。
唱尽新词欢不见，旱云如火扑晴江。

二

秦女端容理玉筝，梁尘踊跃夜风轻。
须臾响急冰弦绝，但见奔星劲有声。

An Untitled Poem

无　题

一九三三年十一月二十七日

一枝清采妥湘灵，九畹贞风慰独醒。
无奈终输萧艾密，却成迁客播芳馨。

Advise Yuh Ta-fu Not to Move His Family to Hangchow

阻郁达夫移家杭州

一九三三年十一月三十日

钱王登假仍如在，伍相随波不可寻。
平楚日和憎健翮，小山香满蔽高岑。
坟坛冷落将军岳，梅鹤凄凉处士林。
何似举家游旷远，风波浩荡足行吟。

An Untitled Poem

无　题

一九三三年十二月三十日

烟水寻常事，荒村一钓徒。
深宵沉醉起，无处觅菰蒲。

Written Jokingly after Reading the Fabricated News about My Suffering from "Meningitis"

报载患脑炎戏作

一九三四年三月十六日

横眉岂夺蛾眉冶，不料仍违众女心。
诅咒而今翻异样，无如臣脑故如冰。

An Untitled Poem

无　题

一九三四年五月三十日

万家墨面没蒿莱，敢有歌吟动地哀。
心事浩茫连广宇，于无声处听惊雷。

Thoughts on an Autumn Night

秋夜有感

一九三四年九月二十九日

绮罗幕后送飞光，柏栗丛边作道场。
望帝终教芳草变，迷阳聊饰大田荒。
何来酪果供千佛，难得莲花似六郎。
中夜鸡鸣风雨集，起然烟卷觉新凉。

To Hsu Kuang-ping
An Inscription on "Chiehtzuyuan's Guide to Traditional Chinese Paintings Vol. 111"

题《芥子园画谱》三集

赠许广平

一九三四年十二月九日

十年携手共艰危，以沫相濡亦可哀。
聊借画图怡倦眼，此中甘苦两心知。

An Impromptu Poem Composed at Late Autumn

亥年残秋偶作

一九三五年十月

曾惊秋肃临天下，敢遣春温上笔端。
尘海苍茫沈百感，金风萧瑟走千官。
老归大泽菰蒲尽，梦坠空云齿发寒。
竦听荒鸡偏阒寂，起看星斗正阑干。

Why I Lost My Love

我的失恋

——拟古的新打油诗

一九二四年十月三日

　　我的所爱在山腰；
想去寻她山太高，
低头无法泪沾袍。
爱人赠我百蝶巾；
回她什么：猫头鹰。
从此翻脸不理我，
不知何故兮使我心惊。

　　我的所爱在闹市；
想去寻她人拥挤，
仰头无法泪沾耳。
爱人赠我双燕图；
回她什么：冰糖壶卢。
从此翻脸不理我，
不知何故兮使我胡涂。

　　我的所爱在河滨；
想去寻她河水深，
歪头无法泪沾襟。
爱人赠我金表索；
回她什么：发汗药。
从此翻脸不理我，
不知何故兮使我神经衰弱。

　　我的所爱在豪家；
想去寻她兮没有汽车，
摇头无法泪如麻。
爱人赠我玫瑰花；
回她什么：赤练蛇。
从此翻脸不理我，
不知何故兮——由她去罢。

Inscription on "Nothing More"

《而已集》题辞

这半年我又看见了许多血和许多泪，

然而我只有杂感而已。

泪揩了，血消了；
屠伯们逍遥复逍遥，
用钢刀的，用软刀的。
然而我只有“杂感”而已。
连“杂感”也被“放进了应该去的地方”时，
我于是只有“而已”而已！

以上的八句话，是在一九二六年十月十四夜里，编完那年那时为止的杂感集后，写在末尾的，现在便取来作为一九二七年的杂感集的题辞。

一九二八年十月三十日，鲁迅校讫记。

Song of the Good Sort

好东西歌

一九三一年十二月十一日

南边整大廾大会，北边忽地起烽烟，
北人逃难南人嚷，请愿打电闹连天。
还有你骂我来我骂你，说得自己蜜样甜。
文的笑道岳飞假，武的却云秦桧奸。
相骂声中失土地，相骂声中捐铜钱，
失了土地捐过钱，喊声骂声也寂然。
文的牙齿痛，武的上温泉，
后来知道谁也不是岳飞或秦桧，
声明误解释前嫌，
大家都是好东西，
终于聚首一堂来吸雪茄烟。

A Nanking Ballad

南京民谣

一九三一年十二月二十五日

大家去谒灵，强盗装正经。
静默十分钟，各自想拳经。

Addendum:

A Lament for Miss Ting

悼 丁 君

一九三三年六月二十八日

如磐夜气压重楼，剪柳春风导九秋。
瑶瑟凝尘清怨绝，可怜无女耀高丘。

Bibliography

Chang Hsiang-tien. *Reference Commentaries on Lu Hsun's Classical Style Poetry.* Canton: People's Publishing House, 1965.

Chou Chen-fu. *Notes to Poems of Lu Hsun.* Chekiang: People's Publishing House, 1962.

Lu Xun: Selected Works. 4 vols. Beijing: Foreign Languages Press, 1980.

Ni Mo-yen. *Preliminary Comments on Lu Hsun's Poems in the Classical Style.* Shanghai: People's Publishing House, 1977.

Pamphlets Concerning Lu Hsun's Poems. Shanghai: The Museum of Lu Hsun in Shanghai, 1973.

Photostatic Reproductions of the Original Handwritten Manuscripts of Lu Hsun's Poems. Peking: Cultural Relics Press, 1976.

Selected Works of Lu Hsun. 4 vols. Peking: Foreign Languages Press, 1964.

Wang Erh-ling. *Reading Notes to Lu Hsun's Classical Poetry.* Tientsin: People's Publishing House, 1979.

Academic journals of the following universities published from 1976 to April 1981:

Nanking University, Peking University, Peking Teachers University, Nankai University, Futan University, Tientsin University, Anhwei University, Sun Yat-sen University, Shantung University, Szechuan Teachers College, etc.